香港國際詩歌之夜 2017
INTERNATIONAL POETRY NIGHTS IN HONG KONG

編輯 Editors

北島 Bei Dao

柯夏智 Lucas Klein

宋子江 Chris Song

逆流而行

安雅．烏德勒

COUNTER POSITION

ANJA UTLER

《逆流而行》
安雅・烏德勒 著

封面影像：北島

國際統一書號（ISBN）：978-988-237-047-0

出版：中文大學出版社
香港 新界 沙田・香港中文大學
傳真：+852 2603 7355
電郵：cup@cuhk.edu.hk
網址：www.chineseupress.com

Counter Position
By Anja Utler

Cover Image: Bei Dao

ISBN: 978-988-237-047-0

Published by The Chinese University Press

The Chinese University of Hong Kong
Sha Tin, N.T., Hong Kong
Fax: +852 2603 7355
E-mail: cup@cuhk.edu.hk
Website: www.chineseupress.com

Printed in Hong Kong

目錄 Contents

安雅・烏德勒
Anja Utler

中文翻譯：歐建梆
English translation by Kurt Beals

entgegen zu stehen:
eine verflechtung in neun teilen

I

ja, wieder und wieder ent-
wrungen sich, immer, bloß
bin murmeln bin: wie
versehrt werden, roh
unterm flimmerhaar,
roh

II

–vernehmen: nur an den schürfstellen: ausgelöst
zerfurchen – stehn, spüren, drifte schon: schlingre dir zu
durchs: zerklüftete höre – du sprichst mir vom
abraum, den halden vom: aufpflanzen,
windrose, -rad vom: rotieren sprichst, glänzendes
rotorblatt sagst du – es: schlingert, ja, schlingre, wie
arm, flügel pflügt: sich den rücken, ja, furcht
durch die erdrauch- die taubnesselfelder
und stumpft: erst am schulterblatt ab

III

– lösen: sich
eingraben –

wie ins wuchernde: einfinden wollen
sich: haspeln, entgegen, sich: auflegen,
-fiedern wie: werden zur: netzhaut
für furchen für flöze und: gänzlich sich
aufspinnen, netznervig werden so
zitternd ein: gitterblick – sehe du
ragst du sprichst – sein wie
hineingewirkt, – wunden: ins
nervenstrang dickicht aus taubnessel
erdrauch; ein pochen – vergesse –
ja höre, vernehme nicht mehr

IV

– entgegen: verspüre nur: taumle, ja, murmle – ein murmelnder
entrinnen – bachlauf, so heißt es – nicht kennen, ja
vielmehr: entgegen zu stürzen sich schließlich
zu: rinnen zu rieseln beginnen ergießen sich
sperrende kiefer bis: tief in die niederung
– talsohle, heißt es – wie: eingeschleust sein
aus dem: speichel- ins bachbett – ent-
lastungsgerinne – entsickert, gemündet in
schlingende flutende; fransen mäandernde
adern sich aus – richtung: talsperre – jochbein, ja
gurgeln und stockt stottert fängt: sich an reusen aus
hornblatt, gezähnt, flutet im: gerodeten mund

V

– stockung – und dennoch: erinnere, nein ich vergesse nicht
teichwirtschaft heißt das ich sehe da hängen
gewässerstufen für karpfen-, forellenzucht aus-
gehoben den winter lang bleiben sie abgelassen
die ufer der schlamm sie starren sie: gleißen im frost
und ich stehe, natürlich, nicht lange dort

VI

– befallen: letztlich: gefallen sein, ja, wie
sich kreuzen –   bestanden besiedelt die: mundhöhle
achsel vom: riedgras der luft über –
frostet, ja, starren – weiß: poche noch –
schon: scharen sporen sich im
geweiteten blick, und bloß: hingespreizt,
klaffe, die firnigen glieder beringt ja: vom reif
von der böschung gehöre schon, gleichsam,
verliere – nur poren mehr – und lieg mir fern

VII

– verweigern:
sich anschmiegen –

verharren noch und: will vergessen zu
sehen zu hören nur: murmeln mehr
vielmals am kiefer der wurzelstock,
fühlbar, der: schlamm in den poren
sie: schuppen sich schorfen – beginnendes
nesselfieber – die nässenden flerne sie
wollen gerinnen zu: rinde zu borke
im wind aus: nordost richtung murmle ich
landmasse tundra – versteppende haut
areale – sie: spreche ich speichle ich
mir in die schürfstellen, wunden, ziel:
lungenflechte statt haar

VIII

– fiebern: beher-
bergt sein –

regelrecht: luftmassen, vielmals hinweg
gefegt übers nässende (...) flügel –
schlägen gleich mitten: ins flimmerhaar,
bleiben, kaum regen sich: ausgeschabt
spröde, so dörrt selbst das: rippenfell,
federnd, von algenschicht rinde bespannt
überwuchert von krustenflechten mit
ihnen in: hungersymbiose – so heißt es –
zu bleiben, dürr aufgesteppt auf den
boden so: mehren sie sich brechen schon
unterm vogeltritt fingerschlag – vielteilig
werden – und krallen sich, staune, ins
bauchfell fest

IX

aufschrecken, schließlich und finde:
den kehlkopf entkernt ist
gehöhlt ihn: betasten die hände,
sie: nesteln, gefiedert, vom
brustkorb ab flechten sich
tiefer ins: schilf schlucken: licht,
gurgeln, dunkel ja, dämmrig
sie: stricken kielwärts ja kehlwärts
sich: hohlräume, mulden aus
halmen aus fingern aus (...)
gleichsam: den dommeln zu – nistplatz,
im singenden rohr heißt es – will wie
verfangen sein – treibgut – vernäht
werden bis in die: stimmritze raschle
fast zittre ich höre dich wieder: sagst
lied sagst du lied – was ist: lied

逆流而行：
連環九部曲

I

一而再，再而三彼此
鬆開彼此，總是坦蕩蕩的
喃喃細語：像是
受傷了，稚嫩地
在纖毛下
稚嫩地

II

——感知：只有在勘探途中：重獲自由

留痕——　站立、感覺，一直飄流：向你

滾動：裂縫在傾聽—你訴說

一堆廢話，一灘渣滓：埋置、

羅盤—訴說輪盤：你說著滾動，閃爍的

它—旋葉：在轉動，正在滾動，如

手臂，如翅膀般犁著：它的背脊，留下車痕

透過地上的煙塵—透過垂死的鳥巢，

並直至：肩甲骨疲態初現

III

——掙脱：　彷彿發瘋似的蔓延：如願出現
挖掘——　在：疾風面前：散開，
如羽毛似地飄著：成長至：視網膜
為留下車痕為鑛層而生，並：全力
快速轉動，神經肌肉變得更發達，更
抖顫：從鐵窗中看出去——看到你
約隱約現，看到你在説話——彷彿
在盤問，在動怒：向著
地上的煙塵中，那神經纖維，那灌木叢裏
垂死的鳥巢；一聲敲打——忘記——
再也無法細聽細察

IV

—— 面 向 ： 只要感覺：搖晃，或細語——那所謂的
逃 脫——　　潺潺溪流—— 不用認識，
只要：俯衝向下，直到
最後：細滴、細漏、傾盆似的落在
人煙罕至的松林，直至：深入下游處
——那人們所稱的波谷——彷彿是：偷偷
的：唾液朝河床洩出——流
走——滲出，流入
彎曲的水流，迂迴曲折的支流
邊緣——朝向：水壩——如顛骨般的水堤，
汩汩地流，跳動，結巴，並困住：陷進魚網的
金魚藻，齒狀的生物，淹沒在：那輪廓分明的
嘴巴之中

V

——停滯—— 然而：我記得，不，我並未忘記
人們所稱為池塘漁業，我看到漂浮在那裏的
水台，用作繁殖鯉魚，鮭魚
整個冬季牠們從岸邊
游至淤泥處，硬邦邦的：在寒霜下閃閃發光
至於我，當然無法長期在那裏佇立

VI

——降臨：　最終：落下，就像是

相遇——　大量聚集，並覆蓋在：口腔，

腋下的：結冰的莎草，極寒的

空氣，它們都僵住了——白茫茫中：仍然悸動的

孢子：成群擠滿在

遼闊的視野之中，純粹：目瞪口呆地

張開四散，那如環狀似的粗糙肢體：隨著

寒霜隨著各自所屬的堤岸，可謂，

失去——只有細孔——我從未曾想過

VII

——拒絕：仍然依舊：想要忘記
假依——　看過的聽過的，只要：多次
從根莖的頷骨中細語著，
清晰可見的：滿佈淤泥的
細孔：剝掉身上的苔蘚——初現的
麻疹——那疼得泣不成聲的瘡口
愈加渾圓：那外皮，那樹皮
在風中打轉，來自：東北大陸的苔原，
我細語著——那塊逐漸蔥郁的
高原——它們：我說著唾涎著
朝著勘探場，朝著傷口，朝著目標：
兜蘚而不是毛髮

VIII

——發燒：完全地：氣團多次的
躲避——　擦過那泣不成聲的（…）雙翼
隨即擺動：在纖毛裏
停留，幾乎靜止不動：被掏空了的
脆弱的，自我榨乾的：胸膜
在伸展著，並為一層層海藻所蓋著，
與殼狀地衣一同茂密地生長
在：人們所稱的——飢餓共生——
枯竭、被縫合
在土地上：它們自我繁殖，在
輕如羽毛的指尖下——形成
多邊形——並牢牢地抓住，目瞪口呆地
凝視著那腹膜壁

IX

最後變得驚愕，發現：
喉頭結去掉
給掏空：雙手輕觸，
它：摸索著，往那羽毛豐滿的
胸腔，深入那
纏繞不清的：蘆葦叢中，吞嚥：輕輕地，
咯咯地，在黑暗中，在薄暮中
它們：往外翻側往空心處插入
編織出：空間，（…）的如手指似的
一株株的波谷
也就是說：朝著麻鴉——築巢的地方，
在那人所稱為歌唱用的簧片——就像是
糾纏不清似地——零碎的殘骸——一針針的
給縫起來，直至：聲門噹啷作響
快要震動我再次聽到你：唸著
歌兒唸著歌兒——那首叫歌兒的歌兒

Counter Position:
An Interweavement in Nine Parts

I

again, then again came un-
wrung, apart, always, bare
am murmur am: as if
wounded, raw
under cilia,
raw

II

—perceive: just at the opencuts: set free
furrow— to stand, sense, to drift now am: pitching to you
through the: fissures hear—you speak of
waste heaps, of scree of: implanting, the
windrose, -wheel speak of: rotating, glistening
rotor blade you say—it: pitches, now, pitch, as a
veined arm, a wing plows: its back, engraves furrows
through earth-smoke through dead nettle fields
and at last: on the shoulder blade dulls down

III

—free from: as if wanting to enter: the wild growth
entrench— to: wind, towards, to: spread,
feather out as: to grow into: retina, network
for furrows for seams and: fully to
spin up, grow nervose so
trembling a: trammeled view—see how you
loom you speak—as if
worked-in, wound-in: to the
nerve-fiber thicket of dead, of deaf nettle of
earth-smoke; a throbbing—forget—
don't listen, perceive any more

IV

—encounter: but feel only: stagger, well, murmur—a
escape— *murmuring*
stream, so it's called—not to know, just
to: plunge down toward finally
to: trickle to drip start to spill over
pinechoked till: deep in the lowland,
—the gullet, it's called—as if: sluiced
from the: spit- to the streambed—*run—*
off—exuded, poured out into
pitching flowing, meandering veins
fray—towards: waterstop—jugal dam,
gurgle and sticks stutters catches:
on snares of
hornwort, toothed, flooding the: clearcut
mouth

V

—stillstand— and yet: remember, no i'm not forgetting
aquiculture it's called i see hanging there
watersteps carved out for carp, for trout
breeding sit drained out all winter
the shore the mud stiffen they: glisten in frost
and i, naturally, don't stand there long

VI

—befall: at last: fallen, to be as if
cross— colonized covered the: cavity, oral,
armpits frosted over with: reed grass with
air, so they, stiffen—white: throb still—
spores: already swarming the
wide-open eyes, only: gaping am
splayed out, the granular limbs so encircled: by frost
by the riverbank already fit, so to speak,
lose—just pores now—lie far from my mind

VII

—refuse: remain still and: want to forget to
nestle to— see to hear just: murmurs now
many times out from the mouth rootstock,
palpable: mud in the pores
they: scale off slough—a nettle rash,
nascent—the weeping sores
want to run thick turn: to rind turn to bark
in the wind from the: tundra i murmur
northeast landmass—skin patches turning
to steppe—they: speak i spit i
into my opencuts, wounds, goal:
lungwort for hair

VIII

—fever: find re-
fuge—

fully: air masses, frequently
swept across weeping (...) wing—
strokes straight: into the cilia,
stay, hardly moving: scraped out
so brittle, that even the: pleura dries,
pliant, coated in algae rind
grown thick with crustaceous lichens
in: hunger symbiosis with them
—so it's called—dry, stitched to the
ground: they multiply break from even
a featherweight fingerstroke—grow multi-
partite—and claw tight, am gaping, into the
abdominal wall

IX

finally, startled from sleep, find:
the larynx deseeded is
hollowed: hands palpate,
it: fumbling, feathered, from
ribcage entwine themselves
deeper into the: reed swallow: light,
gurgling, darkly well, dimly
they: keel towards hulls towards hollows
weave: cavities, gorges of
stalks of fingers of (...)
so to speak: towards the bittern—nesting place,
in the singing reed so it's called—grow
entangled as—flotsam and jetsam—stitched
up to the: glottis rustling
almost trembling i hear you again: say
song you say song—what is: song

Die Lautbildung erfolgt [...] gelegentlich
auch bei Einatmung (inspiratorische Laute).
So wird z.B. als Ausdruck eines plötzlichen,
leichten Schmerzes zuweilen ein
inspiratorisches [f] verwendet.
—R. Arnold / K. Hansen

marsyas, umkreist

weit danach ist:
als rassle als: käme die atmung in gang und
den rand entlang knacken ja platzen die kapseln
die samen sie: spritzen sprühn tiefer, vom
wassersaum ab, übers land

davor:
säumt die zunge den gaumen im zischeln
dem girren dem trillern im (...) in der hitze
verwischt sie – geschnittenes gras – sich
durchschwirrt sie – ein echo – den wind

1

beschattet – umklammern

marsyas, das ist: an den stamm gehangen
bald: ausgelöst sein, an den ast gekrallt – balg –
ist: gespannt, dass die schatten den achseln
entfliehn, von der klinge gespalten zu werden
– der atem gebannt – sehn: sie öffnet das dunkel
gedachte: den strömen aus luft und aus licht

–

so: tasten, die finger, sie wollen: durchschlingen die borke sie
knirscht an den nägeln sie: bricht wie zum: licht hin gelockert
– [kch] – rissig, der rinde zu, drunter das blinde – [ssh] –
sprießende holz quillt vertieft noch – im stillen – den
    dunkelnden kern

–

2

durchtasten – erinnert

–

nur: durchraschelt die: triebe den seidelbast sprossende stängel, die
knospen sind: früh im jahr rosig: gesprungene kelche – so fiebrig
das: birst an den fingern – [ff] – zwittrig – [tss] – fiedrig, durch-
schlungen vom licht das: zur bastschicht zur steinfrucht gerinnt

–

3

säuberlich: scheiden

ihn sich: zu besehen ihm: glänzen die glieder sie
glitschen im schweiß – gekrampft – weißlich vorm
stamm wird das salz: in der achsel ihm ausblühn,
wird starrend, kristallen sein, dann, wenn die hülle
geschrumpft ist vom wind pergamenten daneben
hängt – zapfig im fleisch – das beschaute ab

–

so: binsig die: blattspreite breiten vom sumpfgrund sich: simsen das
schneidried das wiegt: sich die zapfigen ährchen – [ch] – spitzen sie
schneiden das schneidet – [tsh] – zischelt: durchzischelt – die
hornschicht die knospen der fingerbeere – [pfch] – ritzt sich: im wind

–

4

entwuchert – entströmen

striemig, die wölbungen, fasern gelöst aus dem innern
verborgen: so wollten sie keimen die stachelzellen,
hornzellen: sprießende schichten, sie wollten umsäumen
das, was benannt sein soll: zählbare stränge, sie: knospen
den knochen an gräten an: dornigen fortsätzen und
werden abzublättern sein und: sollen rauten – kapuzen –
die bauchmuskeln heißen, zu heben zu senken die rippen
darunter: die lunge, berührbar gemacht, bleibt ein bündel,
vom luftdruck bedrängt

–

geschält: sind sie scharfkantig, blätter: vom rispigen rippigen stiel so
erzittern – [tss] – zwischen den fingern im flötenhals schwingen
erbeben sie spalten: den luftstrom entzweien – [ssh] – säuseln das
röhricht den lippen den rispen gleich teilt sich schwappt: wieder in eins

–

5

strudelnd – veröden

erzittert – die luft von den vögeln durchflohen, durchrauscht –
zu durchfingern die dunkelnden furchen der sage – der
bauchmuskeln nach zu ziehen – zu sehen sie: fiedern, umfiedern
die rippen sind: flügeln gleich wirbeln und strömen darin: irrt der blick
dringt verliert sich im schwindel im schlingen im schaudern im (...)
zusehnds getrieben und schreckt: diese stürzende wunde
der mund: ist vertieft noch und schweigt
– eine plötzliche karste – sich trocknend aus

derweil:

ist entäußert ganz stürzt: er ihm – schließlich – entgegen
und quillt es entgurgelt entkreischt ihm – ein ächzen –
und vorerst nur er: vom entsetzen entbunden wird marsyas wird –
endlich: entströmt er ins harrende land er
entrinnt nicht: entspringt

發音偶然地伴隨[…]
吸氣音(或稱縮氣音)。
例如：吸氣音「f」有時會用作
表示突發性的輕微痛楚。
——R. 阿諾德 / K. 韓森

被包圍的瑪敘阿斯

久而久之：
呼吸彷彿：在噹啷作響，愈來愈多的
種子膠囊沿著縫夾裂開
爆開並：往更遠處濺落四散，從
河邊，散佈大地

之前:
舌頭遲緩地朝上腭挪動，低聲地
咕咕叫著囀鳴著（…）在灼熱的環境中
它混淆了——修剪過的青草——
呼呼地叫著——回音——在風中

1

蒙上陰影——抱緊

瑪敘阿斯：被吊掛在樹幹上
即將：被剝皮，繫在樹枝上的——獸皮——
拉緊，然後刀刃掰開了
從腋下逃脫的影子
——苟延殘喘地——看著：昏暗幻象
初現：空氣與光線流動著

——

然後：指頭感受著，想要：引線入樹皮編織
指甲發出撕裂聲：折斷，彷彿是：光線讓它鬆弛
——[kch]——朝向外皮，並咯擦作響，失明的
在下方——[ssh]——長著嫩芽的木頭膨脹著，
變得更加深沉——在寂寥中——
那發黑的果核

——

2

模索——記憶

——

只要：窸窣地：往茁壯生長的玉桂樹莖發射，
那花蕾：年初是桃紅色的：破裂的聖杯——令人
　　如此亢奮
爆開了：在指頭上——[ff]——雌雄同體的——
　　[tss]——彷似羽毛，被光線
纏繞著：凝結成一層絨毛，核果
——

3

有條不紊：剪斷

他：看著他和他的：肢體在閃爍
汗涔涔卻閃閃發光—— 抽搐著—— 在樹幹前面
白色的鹽佈滿—— 腋下，
如結晶體似的變得堅硬，然後陣風
枯萎它的皮膚，像羊皮紙似的在旁邊
吊掛著—— 血肉之軀在寒氣中—— 被審視

——

因此：苔蘚蔓生的：葉片在沼澤地上張開：蘆葦
香附子搖曳：在結了冰的幼穗叢中—— [ch]—— 刺到它們
剪斷那可剪的—— [tsh]—— 嘶叫著：低聲細語著——
角質層，如指頭般的果肉花蕾—— [pfch]—— 在風中：刮擦著
——

4

蔓延——傾倒

倏痕密佈的腫脹纖維從內部釋放
給遮蔽著：想要發芽，刺狀細胞，
角質細胞：一層一層幼苗渴望繞著
自己即將得到的名字：一定數量的軟線，花蕾：
倚著瘦骨嶙峋的山脊綻放：荊棘不斷往外延伸
而那些所謂菱形、梯形的、
腹部的肌肉：將要脱落，使肋骨能上下移動
在肋骨之下的：赤裸裸的肺部仍然被捆住，
被空氣擠壓

——

外皮給剝掉了：如刀刃般鋒利的葉片：在圓椎花形的，
　　肋骨似的葉柄中
顫抖著——[tss]——夾在手指之間它們在氣管裏擺動
顫動分裂：氣流——[ssh]——私語著那既像雙唇，
又像圓椎花形的蘆葦叢，分開然後脱落：再合而為一

——

5

天旋地轉—— 杳無人煙

顫抖著—— 群鳥劃破氣團掙脫——
撥弄著前鋸肌烏黑的皺紋——
朝腹肌拉扯——看著：羽毛，被毛茸茸地包裹著的
肋骨：如雙翼般迴轉滑行：眼神游移
在滾動中在哆嗦中（…）擠壓、迷失
為視覺所迷，並為之愕然：這些沉澱的傷口
嘴巴：深沉地靜默著
—— 突如其來的岩熔—— 乾透

與此同時：

他給完全剝掉——最後——他墮落：朝向它

並膨脹，它因此發出咯咯聲，嘎吱作響——一聲呻吟——

並只是暫且：解除恐怖魔咒的瑪敘阿斯起了變化——

最後：川流不息穿行在等待中的土地

他無從溜掉：往前躍動

Occasionally sound is also produced
[...] by inhaling (ingressive speech).
E.g. an ingressive [f] is sometimes
used to express a sudden, mild pain.
—R. Arnold / K. Hansen

Marsyas, Encircled

long after:
as if the breath: rattled, caught on and
the capsules the seeds at the borders they crack
they burst open they: spray, scatter deeper, from
waterline, over the land

before:
the tongue edges the palate in whispers
in cooing in trilling in (...) in the heat so
it blurs—cut grass—
whirs through—an echo—the wind

1

shaded—embrace

marsyas, is: hung on the stem
to be flayed, is clawed to the branch—hide—
is: stretched, so the shadows they flee from the
armpits, soon: split by the knife
—breath held—to see: how it opens the dimly
imagined: to streams of air and of light

–

so: fingers, they feel, want to: weave through the bark
scrapes the nails: breaks as if it were: loosed towards the light
—[ghh]—ripped, towards the rind, and beneath it the blind—[ss]—
sprouting wood swells still deepens—in silence—
   the darkening seed

–

2

reach through—remembered

–

just: rustles through: shoots through the spurge laurel sprouting stalks,
buds: early in the year rosy the: chalices opened—so feverish
bursts: on the fingers—[ff]—hermaphrodite—[pff]—featherlike, laced
through by light that: congeals into skin fiber, stonefruit

–

3

cleanly: cut

him: to see him his: limbs glint they
glisten in sweat—cramped—in front of the trunk,
salt will bloom in the: armpit, white,
will be stiff, crystalline, then, when his skin
has been shriveled to parchment by wind beside it
hangs—fibrous—the carved flesh

–

so: reedy the: leafblades they spread from the swampground
 the: sedges the
sawgrass that sways: frozen spikelets—[kh]—prick so they
cut that cuts—[tsh]—hisses: whispers through—
corneal layer the finger buds—[pss]—scores itself: in the wind

–

4

broken out—run out

streaked, the swellings, the fibers released from the inside
enwombed: so they wanted to germinate, prickle-cells,
corneocytes: sprouting layers, they wanted to hem in
what will be named: countable strands, they: bud
on bone ridges: on thorny outgrowths and will
need to be deleaved and: should be called rhomboid, trapezius,
abdominal muscles, to lift and to lower the ribs
underneath is: the lung, now laid bare, but still bundled,
pressed under the air

–

stripped: sharp-cornered, leaves: from the panicled ribbed
stem they tremble—[tff]—between the fingers they swing in
the wind pipe they shake split they sever: the airstream—[ssh]
—whisper the reedbed like lips like the panicles parts then
spills: back into one

–

5

whirling—lay waste

trembles—the air is flown through is swept through by the birds—
finger through trace the darkening furrows serratus abdominal
muscles—they: feather, enfeather the ribs are: like wings whirl and
stream the: eyes wander there press lose themselves in the swirl
in the snare in the shudder the (...) visibly driven stops short: this
precipitous wound the mouth: deepened still silent—a sudden
karst—dries out

meanwhile:
is fully divested he—finally—plunges: towards it
and it wells out it gurgles it screeches out from him—a moan—
and for now just: unbound by the horror turns marsyas turns—
finally: flows out and into the waiting land
does not slip out he: springs forth

Сивилла: выжжена, сивилла: ствол.
Все птицы вымерли, но Бог вошел.
Sibylle: ausgebrannt, sibylle: Stamm.
Die Vögel ausgelöscht, Gott aber kam.
—Marina Cvetaeva

sibylle – gedicht in acht silben

hat die: körner berührt, bloßen augs: bloßen munds ist ent-
zunden, sibylle, sie schaudert, glüht: sand sengt die kuppen die
finger die zunge schlägt funken im körper: loht auf

•

sie: taumelt, sibylle, verfallen dem: rinnenden sand stürzt sie, strömt
– myriaden von poren – durchweht sie durchzuckt sie die sonne – wird:
sonnensturm – murmelt sie spuckt, weiß: sie senkt sich nicht mehr

•

ist: geborsten, sibylle, der: splitter im fleisch ist sie – blutet noch? –
spreißelt – entzweit, klafft: den lippen gleich, strunk – ist: lamelle,
verholzt
sie: durchschneidet das licht, trieft: sie knarzt, das: entquillt

•

sibylle so: gähnt sie, ächzt: schwingen die: stimmlippen, -ritzen sie
kratzen: hinweg übern kalk, scheuern, reißen ein: krater vom
becken zur kehle der: stimmschlund, sibylle, sie: zittert, vibriert

•

vibriert, ist: das beben, sibylle – erschütterung – zuckt: in den sand- in
den luftwirbeln knirscht sie verwirft: das gelenk sich staucht, wimmert: zur
nehrung: verzehrt sie sich – zittert: entwurzelte kiefer – sie: erodiert

•

sibylle sie: türmt sich, wird: klippen sie zischt ist die: gischt in den
poren verglüht sie versprüht: sibilanten, erlischt -sss- ebbt
flutet sich selbst und: stöhnt auf

•

ihr: schwindelt, sibylle sie: bricht sich in wirbelnder hitze sie: zischelt
sirrt: sumpf, tümpel glitschende schenkel der: schilfgürtel nässt sie um-
züngelt sich selbst gurgelt – natter – entwischt sie und: girrt

•

•

und still. bloß die witterung: brandstätte rodung vernehmbar – ist ehemals knistern – und fäulnis: die zehen befingern den strunk: eine pilzige höhlung, bestochern die ab geworfene haut: sie zerfällt an den schuppigen sohlen und: raschelt auf

女預言師：燒至灰燼，女預言師：樹幹
即使鳥兒泯滅，神明依然降臨。
——瑪麗娜・茨維塔耶娃

女預言師——一首八節的詩歌

撫摸了：穀粒，用她赤裸裸的雙眼：點燃著她赤裸裸的
　　嘴巴，
女預言師，她在顫抖、發亮：砂子燒燙整個山頂
指頭舌頭傳遍全身：熊熊地燃燒著

・

她：搖晃著，女預言師，腐化：飛砂落下，她流動
——千變萬化的細孔——狂吹著她灼熱地燃燒著她，太
　　陽——轉化成：
太陽風暴——她耳語著啐著唾沫，明白：它無法再退卻

・

女預言師：支離破碎：碎片嵌在皮膚裏，她——血是否
　　仍然在流？——

碎裂——斬斷，她張著嘴巴：就像嘴唇一樣，樹莖——
　　是：薄板、變成木質
她：斬斷光線，細細滴下：她尖叫著：往前躍動

•

女預言師，因此：打著呵欠，抱怨著：在搖晃的：發出
　　聲音的嘴唇，——它們在刮擦著
劃破：石灰石，它們揉搓著，撕碎一個：從盆地
至食道的石坑：聲喉撕裂，女預言師她：顫動、振動

•

在振動：地震，女預言師——震盪——抽搐：在風沙中
在旋渦中她咬牙切齒她退卻：關節被擠壓、抽泣：在
沙壩：思念著——顫動著：連根拔起的顎骨——她：在
　　腐蝕

•

女預言師：她在堆積著，開始：石崖嘶嘶作響：泡沫從
細孔消隱傾瀉：嗞嗞的聲音遠去 -sss- 旋渦
泛濫然後：嘆息

•

她：頭暈目眩，女預言師她：因席捲而來的熱流而崩潰：| 喃喃自語

嗡嗡叫著：沼澤、池塘、滑溜溜的大腿：她沾濕著蘆葦叢，繞著自己

舌頭咯咯作響——游蛇——她滑溜：咕咕叫著

•

•

然後仍舊：那天然香氣：清晰聽見人們在清理火災現場——

曾經蕭瑟叫著——腐爛：腳趾指向樹幹:

真菌狀植物中空，探索脫落的外皮：在鱗片密佈的

腳掌上腐化，然後：沙沙作響

Sibyl: in cinders, Sibyl: a trunk.
The birds incinerate, but God has come.
—Marina Cvetaeva

Sibyl—Poem in Eight Syllables

has touched the: grains, with her naked eye: naked mouth en-
kindled, sibyl, she shudders, she glows: the sand singes the finger
tips tongue it strikes sparks in the body: flares up

•

she: staggers, sibyl, struck down to: the sand falls she, streams
– myriads of pores – blasts through now flashes through sibyl the
sun – turns to:
sunstorm – she murmurs she spits, knows: it no longer sets

•

has: burst open, sibyl, the: splinter in flesh is she: bleeding still? –
tinders – is severed, she gapes: like the lips, stump – is: lamella,
lignified
slices: the light, drips: she screeches it: springs forth

•

sibyl so: yawns so she, sighs: vocal lips, folds: they swing they
scrape: off over limestone, they scrub, rip a: crater from
basin to gullet the: voicecleft, so sibyl, she: oscillates, shakes

•

shaken: the quaking is, sibyl – shock – lurches: in sand eddies
air eddies gnashes she throws out: her joint buckles, wails so she: pines
wastes away to: spit, sand bar she – oscillates: uprooted jaw – she:
erodes

•

sibyl she: towers up, turns to: cliffs hisses is: spindrift glows out in the
pores sprays out: sibilants, goes out -sss- ebbs
surges swells and: suspires

•

sibyl her: head swims, she: breaks in the swirling heat: whispers,
she whirs: sump, slough slick thighs: the reed belt she wets she en-
girds herself tongues gurgles – adder – she slips off and: sisses

•

•

and still. just the scent: fire site clearing to hear – once
a rustling – and spoilage: toes finger the stump:
fungous hollow, they probe cast-off skin: it breaks down
on the scaled soles and: crackles out

Im Lorbeer gewährt die verwandelte Daphne,
deren Name selbst den Lorbeer bezeichnet,
sich dem zum Dichter gewordenen Liebenden.
—Karlheinz Stierle

Der Seidelbast ist wie andere Daphnearten sehr stark
giftig. [...] Die Blätter ähneln im Aussehen denen des
Lorbeerbaumes, daher der Gattungsname Daphne.
—Eintrag unter www.heilpflanzen-suchmaschine.de

für daphne: geklagt

mir selbst: wie entstachelt! von ihm als: habe sich alles
gedreht bin: gewittert, gepirscht jetzt – ganz: der gehetzte
schweiß – schnell ich: durch äste, gestrüpp ihm entstürzen
die: fangen zu greifen an haken gepeitscht mir – schneller –
die flanken augen – nein – (...) weiß: ich muss durch da muss
– schleunigst – hin an den fluss, fluss –

–

bitten ihn: nimm mich kurz, vater, ich: tunke mich dir
in die schnellen und du dann: entlasse mich – rein – als die gischt

ja: als luft, luft –
und ich kraus dir entfliehend als dank das gesicht –

–

ja, schon: spritzt du triffst: mir die fesseln – frischst –
wirst mich lösen, lassen – gleich, sofort –

–

darf doch nicht – nein –
was: nimmst du dir –
selber – geradewegs – dir: auf den stickigen grund
gelaufen, festgesetzt: mit einem zug, ruck, nein,
reiße noch bäume mich einmal und stock –
muss: mich krümmen, ja kümmern: ins holz hinein
starren – was nimmst du mir: mich

–

sehe, als letztes: das schmückt dich jetzt, ja, mein
erblindetes bild wird, muss immer, gekraust, mit dir glitzern
und trüber, ja linsig: so schwimmt es – dein dank –
auch dem treiber im blick

–

wie trocken: mein arm macht – machte: die flanken – wie oft –
aufsprudeln, aus-
jetzt: nagen die, speicheln – bespringend – mich an –
machen platz dann: rankt er sich mir zu: und sein heißes fleisch –
feucht! fortwährend – richtest dich auf in mir, mich:
dass ich stehe ja blühe und trage darf: nichtmal die blätter
lassen, mir fallen: nur früchte ab – unwillkürlich: so bring ich die –
rotten, nähren: dir deinen grund

–

weiter nur kümmern, dörren nur: dürsten zu dürfen
hören: ich raschle den vögeln jetzt trockener nach –

senge! bitte, dürre den schatten ihm: von dieser roten stirn,
dass er: ausglüht – ja mir: diesen puls aus den spitzen,
dass ich mich: auslöse – rein – als geruch als entknisternde
luft mich einsenke einsinke – laubend entlaubend mich –
in: die niedrigen, bastigen triebe und sie: enttreibe mir
kirschig, ja gischtig entstrecke – aufzischle: iss davon, iss –

達芬妮幻化成一棵月桂，
用她的名字代表月桂，
並把自己獻給成為她戀人的詩人。
——卡爾海因茨・施蒂爾勒

月桂彷彿是另類品種的達芬妮，
毒性甚強。[…] 葉片跟
月桂樹的葉片甚為相像，因此
屬性亦稱為達芬妮。
文章取自 www.heilpflanzen-suchmaschine.de

為達芬妮：哭號

我自己：荊棘像脫掉了！給他彷彿：一切
都已經在流轉：現在變得香味撲鼻、匍匐而行——完
　　全地：倉皇而生的汗水——我急忙地——穿過枝
　　條，穿過草叢，他們朝他
發光：抓住，如鈎般捆住——愈加快速地——
我的兩脇、雙眼——不對——（…）我知道：我必須
　　跨越它然後往前——立刻——直至到處那河川，
　　那河川——

——

請他：快來接我，爸爸，我：在急流中泡進
你的懷裏，然後你：放開我——自然得——像泡沫
像空氣，對，像空氣——
而我在逃脫中途在你的臉龐上泛起漣漪連聲道謝——

——

然後你已經：傾瀉輕輕拍打我的腳踝——清涼的——
放開我，放任我——現在立刻——

——

也許未能——不——
你手拿著的：究竟是甚麼——
你逕自——奔馳在：透不過氣的土地上，
始終如一：突然一動，傾倒，不，
一棵棵樹的樹幹把我捆住——
我必須：彎著身子，乾癟著，活下去：在樹叢中
堅定地看著——你從我拿走的：我

——

看，像以最後的目光似地：你現在是如何給潤色，對，我

那暗淡的畫像必須永遠蕩漾，與你閃閃發亮
漸漸昏暗，然後呈晶體狀：你的謝禮——遊走著
在獵人的目光下

——

多麼的乾涸：我的手臂變得——變了：兩脇經常——起
　　泡，由外——
現在：啃著，唾涎著——朝著我——攀登——
那麼讓出空間：任他纏繞我：他灼熱的肉身——
潮濕！接二連三——你向著我矗立，抬起我：
而我則時而站立，時而開花，或時而忍受著：不讓
葉片：只是果實落下——不情願地：我因此把它們——
那腐爛的養分：帶到你的土地

——

現在只管：讓其枯萎，口渴
聽著：我讓鳥兒現在更乾巴巴的沙沙叫著——

燒焦吧！請，烤乾他的影子：這紅色的眉毛，
讓他：耗盡所有——從我的——指尖下這脈搏，

讓我：能釋放自己——天然地——像香氣像撕裂的
空氣淹沒沉到水裏——我的葉子生長脱落——
在：矮小的、毛茸茸的幼苗中，他們：離開我，
結著莓類的果實，傾瀉著伸展著——嘶嘶作響：吃在
　　其中，吃著

Transformed into a laurel, Daphne, whose own name denotes the laurel, yields herself to the lover turned poet.

—Karlheinz Stierle

The spurge laurel, like other species of Daphne, is highly poisonous. [...] The leaves resemble those of a laurel tree, hence the genus name Daphne.

—Entry at www.heilpflanzen-suchmaschine.de

For Daphne: Lamented

myself: as if dethorned! by him as: if it had all
turned now am: scented, am stalked—fully: quarry my
sweat—rush: through branches, through brushwood, from
  him
they light: into grab hook whipping—swifter—
my flanks eyes—no—(...) know: i must go through must
make it—at once—to the river, river—

–

beg him: take me quick, father, i: plunge in your
rapids and you then: release me—pure—as foam

as air, air—

and fleeing i ripple your face in thanks—

–

and, already: you spray: lap my ankles—refreshing—

will free me, let go—now, at once—

–

may not though—no—

what: are you taking—

to you, ran—straight—onto your: sodden

ground, fixed: with a single jerk, lurch, no,

limbs ripping still rear up and stop—

i must: warp myself, withered, worked into the wood

stiffen—what are you taking from me: me

–

see, as last sight: it adorns you, my

unseeing image will, must always, glitter with you, rippled,

dimmer, now skimming: your thanks now—it swims—

in the eyes of the hunter as well

–

how dry: my arm makes—made! the flanks, often, now they
well up, out
they: salivate, gnaw—at me—mounting—
make room then: entwines himself in me: and his hot flesh—
damp! so unceasing—you rise up in me, raise me:
that i may stand, bloom and bear may: not even shed
leaves, just my: fruits fall away—unawares: so i bring them they—
rot, nourish: your ground

–

now allowed just to wither, to parch just: to thirst
hear: i rustle out drier now after the birds—

singe! please, scorch the shadow from him: from this red brow,
so that he: may burn out—this pulse: from my tips,
so that i may: release myself—pure—as a scent as uncrackling
air may submerge may submerse—myself leafing deleafing—
into: the low, spurging shoots: drive them from me
berried, spraying, stretch out—hissing: eat of it, eat—

安雅・烏德勒(德國),1973年生於施萬多夫,現往返於維也納、布拉格和雷根斯堡三地。她在維也納應用藝術大學教授詩歌,她的丈夫在布拉格,她的書在雷根斯堡。2003年,她在雷根斯堡大學取得博士學位,研究題目為俄國現代主義詩歌。2003年,詩集*münden – entzüngeln*贏得Leonce-und-Lena-Preis詩歌獎。英譯詩集*engulf – enkindle*入選2012年最佳翻譯書獎決選名單。她最近的著作*ausgeübt. Eine Kurskorrektur*探討與生態學有關的政治議題,該書獲得2014年巴塞爾詩歌獎。2014年,參加愛荷華大學國際寫作計劃。2015年春天,在美國俄亥俄州歐柏林學院任駐校德語作家。烏德勒的詩集*brinnen*(2006)和*jana vermacht*(2009)都以書籍和聲音檔案兩種形式出版,後者更改變成裝置藝術展覽。

Anja Utler (Germany) was born in Schwandorf in 1973, and currently shuttles between Vienna, where she teaches poetry at the University of Applied Arts, Prague, where her husband lives, and Regensburg, where her books are. In 2003 she received her PhD at the University of Regensburg with a dissertation on Russian Modernist poetry. Her poetry collection *münden – entzüngeln* won the coveted "Leonce-und-Lena-Preis" for Poetry in 2003. The American translation by Kurt Beals, *engulf – enkindle*, was a Best Translated Book Award finalist in 2012. For her innovative poetic exploration of political issues such as ecology in her latest book *ausgeübt. Eine Kurskorrektur*, she was awarded with the "Basler Lyrikpreis" (Basel Poetry Prize) in 2014. She is Honorary Fellow of the International Writing Program of the University of Iowa (IWP '14), and in spring 2015, she was German Writer in Residence at Oberlin College, Ohio. Utler's works explore the impact of different media and modes of perception on the experience of a text: her works *brinnen* (2006) and *jana, vermacht* (2009) were both published in print and audio formats; *jana, vermacht* was also transformed into an installation for an exhibition. Poems by Anja Utler have been translated into numerous languages.

香港國際詩歌之夜 2017
International Poetry Nights in Hong Kong 2017

主辦單位 Organizers

香港中文大學文學院
Faculty of Arts, The Chinese University of Hong Kong
香港詩歌節基金會有限公司
Hong Kong Poetry Festival Foundation Limited

協辦單位 Co-organizers

香港中文大學中國文化研究所
Institute of Chinese Studies, The Chinese University of Hong Kong
香港中文大學出版社
The Chinese University Press
香港大學美術博物館
The University Museum and Art Gallery, The University of Hong Kong
香港大學文學院
Faculty of Arts, The University of Hong Kong
香港科技大學賽馬會高等研究院
Jockey Club Institute for Advanced Study, Hong Kong University of Science and Technology
香港科技大學人文學部
Division of Humanities, Hong Kong University of Science and Technology
廣州時刻文化傳播有限公司
Moment Communications
活字文化
MoveableType Legacy (Beijing) Co., Ltd.
當當
DANGDANG

贊助 Sponsors

中國會 The China Club
北京匡時國際拍賣有限公司 Beijing Council International Auction Co., Ltd.
先鋒公益基金會 UCF Charity Foundation Limited
卓爾書店 the zall bookstore
斑馬谷文化發展有限公司 Zebra Valley Culture Development
馮鑫牟希文夫婦 Feng Xin (Larry) and Mu Xi Wen (Maggie)
蓮華書院 Lianhua Academy